A

Literature Unit

for

Dragon's Gate

by Laurence Yep

Written by Mary Thomas-Vallens

Teacher Created Materials, Inc.
P.O. Box 1040
Huntington Beach, CA 92647
©1996 Teacher Created Materials
Made in U.S.A.
ISBN 1-55734-814-6

Illustrated by
José L. Tapia
Cover Art by
Wendy Chang

Table of Contents

Introduction

Throughout our lives, there are many things we take for granted. Getting from one place to another, for instance, is something most of us do without thinking about the origins of travel. The means of transportation we have is the result of the blood, sweat, and tears of those who came before us. Books can open our eyes to those things we take for granted — to the struggles and hardships that others have experienced in order to make our lives better.

Through reading, we can witness the experiences of others. We can widen our perspective to encompass the lives of those who endured more than we can ever imagine. As books broaden our awareness, we can learn more about ourselves and the world in which we live. *Dragon's Gate* is a book that will have a lasting impact on its readers.

In *Literature Units*, we have searched for novels that not only entertain but provide us with greater knowledge and understanding of our own humanity.

Teachers who use this unit will find the following features to supplement their own valuable ideas.

- Sample Lesson Plan

- Pre-reading Activities

- A Bibliographical Sketch and Picture of the Author

- A Book Summary

- Vocabulary Lists and Suggested Vocabulary Activities

- Chapters grouped for study into section activities which include:

  -quizzes

  -hands-on projects

  -cooperative learning activities

  -cross-curricular activities

  -extensions into the reader's own life

- Post-reading Activities

- Book Report Ideas

- Research Ideas

- Culminating Activities

- Three Different Options for Unit Tests

- Bibliography of Related Reading

- Answer Key

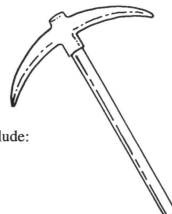

We are confident this unit will be a valuable addition to your planning, and we hope your students' lives will be positively affected by their involvement with *Dragon's Gate.*

Sample Lesson Plan

Each of the lessons suggested below can take from one to several days to complete.

Lesson 1 — Pre-reading Activities

- Introduce the novel by completing some or all of the pre-reading activities. (page 5)
- Read "About the Author" with your students. (page 6)
- Introduce the vocabulary list for Section 1. (page 8)
- Discuss the "Vocabulary Activity Ideas." (page 9) Use this worksheet to vary the vocabulary study activities that you assign to the class.

Lesson 2 — Section 1 Activities

- Assign the vocabulary list for Section 1. (page 8)
- Read and discuss "Preface" in *Dragon's Gate.* Define "genocide" and "reprisals." Discuss paragraphs three and four to set the stage for the Chinese departure to America.
- Define point of view — first and third person. Have students skim page 1 to determine the point of view in which the story is told.
- Read chapters 1–3 and complete the top section of "Quiz Time." (page 10)
- Do "Reasons for Immigration." (page 14)
- Read chapters 4–6 and have students finish the bottom section of "Quiz Time." (page 10)
- Model and assign "Character Analysis" chart. (pages 12–13)
- Do "Act It Out." (page 11)
- Begin "Reader's Response Journal." (page 15)

Lesson 3 — Section 2 Activities

- Assign the vocabulary list for Section 2. (page 8)
- Introduce "Culture Clues" worksheet (page 18). Have students look for examples as they read.
- Discuss what it means to be adopted and the search for identity that adopted children commonly experience.
- Read chapters 7–9, and complete the top section of "Quiz Time." (page 16)
- Do "Culture Clues" (page 18). Students may also add details to their "Character Analysis" and "Reasons for Immigration" worksheets.
- Read chapters 10–12 and have students finish the bottom section of page 16.
- Make a picture postcard. (page 17)
- Discuss status. (pages 19–20)
- Have students write using "Express Yourself." (page 21)

Lesson 4 — Section 3 Activities

- Assign the vocabulary list for Section 3. (page 8)
- Read chapters 13–15 and complete the top section of "Quiz Time." (page 22)
- Make Chinese rice and use chopsticks. (page 23)
- Build cabin models. (page 24)
- Read chapters 16–18 and finish the bottom section of "Quiz Time." (page 22)
- Learn about idioms. (page 25)
- Discuss and interview others about the strength of the human spirit. (page 26)

Lesson 5 — Section 4 Activities

- Assign the vocabulary list for Section 4. (page 8)
- Read chapters 19–21 and complete the top section of "Quiz Time." (page 27)
- Explore blindness. (page 28)
- Examine the first lines, last lines, and titles of books. (page 29)
- Read chapters 22–24 and complete the bottom section of "Quiz Time." (page 27)
- Write a news story about an avalanche. (page 30)
- Share your dreams. (page 31)

Lesson 6 — Section 5 Activities

- Assign vocabulary list from Section 5. (page 8)
- Read chapters 25–27 and complete the top section of "Quiz Time." (page 32)
- Share your treasure. (page 33)
- Do "Words with Multiple Meanings." (page 35)
- Read chapters 28–30 and finish the bottom half of "Quiz Time". (page 32)
- Analyze the story line of the novel. (page 34)
- Take a stand or debate an issue. (page 36)

Lesson 7 — Post-reading Activities

- Discuss any questions your students have about the novel.
- Assign a book report and/or research activity. (pages 37–38)
- Begin work on one or more of the culminating activities. (pages 39–41)

Lesson 8 — Assessment

- Administer unit tests 1, 2, and/or 3. (pages 42–44).
- Encourage students to explore related topics further. (page 45)

Before the Book

Before reading *Dragon's Gate*, help students become familiar with the time period and the cultural background of the Chinese immigrating to the United States of America to work on the transcontinental railroad.

> **Note to the teacher:** For ease of reference, page numbers from *Dragon's Gate* have been included throughout this unit. The referenced pages apply to the 1993 Scholastic version of the novel. Page numbers for subsequent paperback or hard bound publications may vary.

The following activities will help build such an understanding, and will increase interest into reading the novel.

1. Have students use all possible clues from the book cover to make predictions about the novel. Ask them to use the book title, cover illustrations, and the book cover description to make predictions about the novel. Record these predictions on butcher paper. Have students refer to these predictions from time to time throughout the novel study to compare their pre-reading ideas to what actually happens in the story.

2. Discuss other books by Laurence Yep that students may have read.

3. Define and discuss historical fiction. Ask students how reading a fictional account of real situations can enhance our understanding of history.

4. Use a map of China, a world map, and a map of the United States to explore the settings of the story (China and U.S.). Locate China and the United States on a map, and then discuss the following:

   • If a person were to immigrate from China to the United States by ship, what would be the most likely route?

   • What effect does immigration have on our country? (new ideas, new products, conflicts)

   • The book focuses on the building of the transcontinental railroad in the United States during the mid-1800s. What does *transcontinental* mean?

   • What importance would a transcontinental railroad have to a country?

5. Have students gather pictures of China and the United States during the mid-1800s. Have them look for similarities and differences in the two lands. Ask students to read about China in an encyclopedia or ask friends/family of Chinese descent for cultural and historical information about China.

6. Examine one of the novel's key themes: immigration and what drives a person to leave his or her homeland for a strange, new place. Have students speculate about the following:

   • What entices people to give up all that they have to move somewhere else?

   • Why are people willing to leave friends and family?

   • What conditions at home force or encourage people to leave their homelands?

   • Why are people willing to take such risks?

About the Author

Laurence Yep, a highly acclaimed writer, was born in San Francisco on June 14, 1948. For many years while growing up, he lived in an apartment over the grocery store his father and mother owned. They worked twelve hours a day for seven days a week, so life revolved around the store. His working-class neighborhood was racially and ethnically mixed. His years working at the store gave him experience with people of many backgrounds, ideas for his writing, and the discipline to work long hours on his novels.

As described in his memoirs, titled *The Lost Garden*, Yep's caring parents spent many hours reading to him and making literature one of his greatest pleasures. He describes struggling in sports, even though his father was a great coach in town. His mother would make time in her busy schedule to take Laurence to Golden Gate Park, the zoo, the aquarium, De Young Museum, and the beach. Yep loved these outings and also loved the "trips" he took in his mind. His imagination was vivid from a very young age.

As a first generation Chinese-American, Laurence Yep grew up juggling the two cultures in which he was immersed. He just wanted to be an all-around American boy, but he found life growing up in the city, just outside Chinatown, was not that simple. His writing often reflects a search for identity and a feeling of being treated as an outcast.

Racism and prejudice were issues that Mr. Yep had to endure. When he attended a mostly white boy's high school, some students were surprised that Laurence knew English. Often it was not fully realized by others that he was an American, born and raised in the same town, speaking their same language. When playing soldiers and war games, he played the Korean or Chinese-Communist who got "killed," which added to his feeling of isolation.

Laurence Yep had some wonderful science and English teachers at St. Ignatius High School in San Francisco. He enjoyed playing pranks with his experiments, but also found joy in learning to write. He won awards in both fields, but he gradually realized that writing allowed him the freedom to use his imagination and to take elements from his youth and incorporate them into his own stories. Writing also served as a vehicle for sorting out his own identity and gave him a better understanding of who he is.

Laurence Yep's literary works include *Sweetwater, Child of the Owl, Kind Hearts and Gentle Monsters, Dragon of the Lost Sea, The Serpent's Children, Dragon Steel, Mountain Light, The Rainbow People,* and *Dragonwings*, a Newbery Honor Book.

Dragon's Gate

by Laurence Yep

Scholastic, 1993

(Available in Canada from Scholastic, in UK from Scholastic Limited, and in Australia from Ashton Scholastic-Party Limited)

In July of 1865, two men are given heroes' welcomes as they return from America. Uncle Foxfire and Father bring news of their travels. They create a driving urge in their teenaged nephew and son, Otter, to follow them to America. Uncle Foxfire wants to save China from the opium use that is ruining his country. In what he describes as the "Great Work," Foxfire sees America as the answer to his country's needs. He hopes to learn about the railroad and other technological advances and bring them home to China. Taken by his uncle's passion and his goals, Otter wishes to go to America with Father and Foxfire.

Otter visits Dragon's Gate, a place where people make wishes. He makes his wish to go to America, not realizing the fate that wish will bring.

After an arduous voyage, Otter and other Chinese immigrants arrive in America. They soon learn that they are the Americans' cheap labor force, and they must endure horrendous conditions. The men are to break a railroad tunnel through the mountain the men call Snow Tiger.

Otter is angered by the false impressions Foxfire and Father unwittingly created about America. Until he is whipped by the boss, Kilroy, he cannot understand why the men are unable to change their situation.

An explosion in the mountain tunnels takes the sight of Father, and an avalanche traps Chinese workers who are left to die. Kilroy takes no pity on the men and pushes them hard. Otter and the men sink lower and lower into despair.

The threat of another avalanche is imminent. In what is their most daring mission, Otter, Foxfire, and Kilroy's son, Sean, climb the mountain to set off explosives hoping to force the avalanche away from the cabins. An injury forces Sean back, but the uncle and his nephew continue. On the mountain's summit, Otter discovers that Foxfire is indeed a great man. Foxfire is injured in the freezing snow, but Otter successfully sets off the explosives and saves the men below. Otter, delirious and sick with hypothermia, returns to the cabins. Meanwhile, Foxfire secretly hides away to die so that Otter can survive the way back, unburdened by his fallen uncle.

With the help of all the men, Otter is nursed back to health. Even when he is allowed to leave the mountain, Otter chooses to stay to find his Uncle's bones and continue the "Great Work" Foxfire hoped to achieve. No longer the weak boy he once was, Otter leads the men in a strike, and stays on to finish the railroad.

Vocabulary Lists

Because the context provides clues to a word's meaning, page numbers have been provided so students can locate the words in the book. Knowing the context is essential, as many of these words are used in uncommon ways.

Section 1 (Preface to Chapter 6)

agent	12	diligence	8	penitently	29	revolutionary	17
banish	17	genocide	(preface)	pillaged	16	sporadic	2
chagrin	4	insolent	3	prophet	20	stiletto	42
courier	37	ironical	23	refuge	15	subscription	2
defied	12	lavished	9	reprisals	(preface)	tithe	24

Section 2 (Chapters 7–12)

claustrophobic	70	escorts	53	provisions	63	sardonically	84
cur	84	hazed	103	quelling	67	sledges	59
dialect	79	menacingly	89	queue	79	swathed	88
dirge	75	preposterous	67	retaliatory	58	vehemently	89
disembarked	53	propriety	82	sanitation	53	vengeful	100

Section 3 (Chapters 13–18)

brigands	140	disconcerting	124	province	115	sidle	121
conspiracy	131	feint	137	pungent	128	synchronized	157
contemptuously	147	jauntily	122	rapport	114	tirade	138
daguerreotype	139	limned	123	refrained	115	wistful	128

Section 4 (Chapters 19–24)

coherent	183	enunciated	172	lacerated	178	sullen	178
complexion	203	insulation	185	recognition	200	taunted	209
crevasse	212	intrepid	208	redistributed	211	unrepentant	166
deftly	210	irrational	170	scrounge	185	wrath	179

Section 5 (Chapters 25–30)

beacon	257	forfeit	242	obscene	250	skulked	260
caterwauling	252	impale	230	obscuring	231	subscription	269
deliriously	232	lilting	252	pivoted	216	surly	245
diminutive	228	magistrate	269	placard	249	tactics	216
drubbing	259	mementos	237	recruit	224	teamster	245
executioner	229	nitroglycerine	245	significance	251	tourniquet	228

Vocabulary Activity Ideas

Vocabulary Study

1. Choose words that are new or interesting to you.
2. Write each word with the page number where it can be found in the book.
3. Do the activity or activities that your teacher has checked off for you to do:
   - Definitions (Use the dictionary to help you define the word.)
   - Sentences in Context (Write a sentence using the vocabulary word in such a way that the word's meaning becomes clear in the sentence.)
   - Sentence Search (Find the word in the book, copy its sentence, and underline the word.)
   - Synonyms and Antonyms (Write words that mean the same and/or ones that mean the opposite of the words you choose.)

Figurative Language and Common Expressions

Recognizing the author's use of figurative language and idiomatic expressions will help you appreciate the richness of the written word. Find passages that contain vivid figures of speech. These include similes, metaphors, idioms, and personification. Understanding what these figures of speech mean is essential to comprehending the story.

Simile — a clearly defined comparison of two or more essentially unlike things. The comparison is made in the sentence using the words "like" or "as."

Examples: Her skin was as white as snow. The rocket soared through the sky like a bird.

Metaphor — an implied comparison in which one thing is called another.

Example: When my dad is angry, he's a bear.

Personification — a description where inanimate objects, ideas, or animals are given human qualities.

Example: The children felt the cave's darkness would swallow them up forever.

Idioms — a phrase or expression that is commonly used in language, but cannot be explained by its literal meaning and is peculiar to that language; dialect.

Example: Please make the bed.

Extra Credit: "Show, Not Tell"

"Show, Not Tell" is a writing technique where the author uses description to "paint" a mind picture for the reader. The author "shows" the reader by writing specific details to create the image, rather than simply "telling" the reader in short, nondescript terms. Often similes, metaphors, personification and/or idioms are used in "show, not tell" descriptions. Find good examples of show, not tell writing that you would like to share with others.

(Note to the teacher: Due to the complexity of the story, you may want students to read and answer chapters 1–3 questions after reading that part of the book, and save the remaining questions until chapters 4–6 have been read. Have students write responses on separate paper.)

Quiz Time

Chapters 1–3

1. Why does Otter buy toys and treats for everyone at his school?

2. How does Otter's family and village feel about the Manchus? Why?

3. What is the "Work" or "Great Work" that is often mentioned thus far? How do you think Otter feels about the Great Work?

4. What is "demon mud"? What effect has it had on the people of China? (pages 16–17) What examples have been given?

5. Reread the last three paragraphs on page 17. Explain what is being described.

6. Describe how Uncle Foxfire plans to carry out the Great Work.

7. What is Otter's dilemma about going to the Golden Mountain with his father and uncle?

8. Otter says to his father, "Why don't you step out from Uncle's shadow for once?" What does this mean? What is Father's response?

Chapters 4–6

Reminder: Words written in italics in the novel are those words spoken in English. All other dialogue is in Chinese.

9. What is the fateful wish that Otter makes at Dragon's Gate? (page 39)

10. In this section, the title's meaning is revealed. What is "Dragon's Gate"?

11. Write what you think the following quotation means: "Be careful what you wish, for it may come true."

12. Tell how and why the accident happened. Tell how Otter and his friend got away.

13. What do these quotes from Otter mean: "In the back of my mind I began to wonder what I really was."... "but I felt as if a door were being unlocked inside."

14. How does Otter feel now that he has his wish?

(**Note to the teacher**: The activities on this page will work best if done after the cooperative learning "Character Analysis" activity for chapters 1–6. Make sure students have read at least chapters 1–4.)

Act It Out

"I hear and I forget. I see and I remember. I do and I understand."

—Old Chinese Proverb

When you read the novel, you see the words and, hopefully, remember them. For deeper understanding, you need to become actively involved in the story. In this series of activities, you will "become" one of the main characters of the story. You will use what you have learned about the main characters and then create your own role-playing skit or readers' theater presentation.

Otter feels a growing inner struggle in trying to satisfy both his mother's and his uncle's wishes. Otter is like the rope in a tug of war, with his mother pulling on one side and his uncle tugging at the other side.

Activities

1. **Draw a Venn diagram** (two large circles with a small overlapping area) on a piece of paper. In one, write "Mother," and in the other, write "Uncle Foxfire." In each circle, write what the character wants Otter to do.   The overlap will be for any items that are not in conflict — the wishes for Otter that Mother and Uncle Foxfire both share. Discuss your diagram with your partner or class.

2. **Create a simple performance.**

   • Reread pages 32–36 of the book, starting with "I had been looking forward to this moment . . ." Notice the conversations between Mother, Father, Uncle Foxfire, and Otter.

   • Perform a skit by having class members take the roles of Mother, Father, Uncle Foxfire, Otter, and Narrator (shares Otter's feelings). For a readers' theater, recite these parts in unison.

   • Use pages 32–36 of the novel to create the script for your skit or readers' theater presentation. Have the script reflect the mental tug of war Otter is experiencing between Mother and Uncle Foxfire. Show how Father is afraid to share his true feelings.

   • Using your script, perform the words of Mother, Father, Uncle Foxfire, Otter/Narrator (says what Otter is thinking), and Otter. This reading will help emphasize the "tug of war" that Otter feels.

   • If time allows, create simple props that can be used by the characters to best represent who they are.

> By *"doing,"* your understanding of the story will deepen.

Character Analysis

Otter is greatly influenced by two important people in his life: his adoptive mother Cassia, and Uncle Foxfire. Even though Otter is considered a "Stranger," his adopted mother has raised Otter as one of her own clan after the loss of his parents. Her ideas are strong and clear, but as Otter grows up, he has different dreams and wishes for his life. Otter loves Cassia, but he looks toward his future in ways that are sometimes in conflict with her goals.

Uncle Foxfire has been to the Golden Mountain and back. He brings a vision of the future that is exciting and noble, one that will bring greatness to China. Otter admires his uncle greatly. The image he holds of his uncle leads Otter to take an unexpected path in his life.

To better understand Otter and his life, it is important to understand Cassia and Uncle Foxfire. While reading, look for the descriptions, words, and actions of these two people. With a partner or team, record them and the pages on which you found them. Use the spaces below and on page 13. (You may record actual quotes or summarize your findings into your own words.) Next, tell what you think your descriptions or quotes reveal about the person. You may have some team members record information for Mother and others record information for Uncle Foxfire. Then, compare notes with one another.

For the first chapter, quotes and descriptions have been provided for you. Tell what you think they mean.

Mother — Cassia

Descriptions, Words, Actions (page)

1. generous with everyone but herself, "too impatient to be carried in sedan chair," (page 4)

2. "still has mud between her toes" (page 4)

3. "tugging self-consciously at her jade necklace. . . her one piece of jewelry. . . pants were clean but plain" (page 4)

4. "frowned 'Dirty Already'. . . seized arm. . . brushed off my clothes as if I were still a child" (page 4)

Reader's Interpretations

_____

_____

_____

_____

_____

_____

_____

_____

_____

_____

_____

Character Analysis (cont.)

Mother — Cassia (cont.)

5. always stopped to explain why she adopted — born in hour of fire — destined to join family of rebels and troublemakers (page 5)

_____
_____

6. believed in the Great Work — to bring harmony and peace to Middle Kingdom — states that is the reason Otter, Father, and Uncle are on this earth (page 6)

_____
_____

7. disapproved of Rock Lady's elaborate hairstyle; was ready to give her lecture on waste (pages 7–8)

_____
_____

Uncle Foxfire

Descriptions, words, actions (page)   **Reader's Interpretations**

8. "while Father and Uncle were home, life was one long festival..." (page 4)

_____
_____

9. first to leave Three Willows 10 years ago; famous for finding gold where no one else could (page 6)

_____
_____

10. fairy tales of him flying, killing tigers barehanded, calling upon dragons as friends (page 6)

_____
_____

11. "Mother said it was intelligence and not magic that had created his success" (page 6)

_____
_____

12. "And somehow I pictured that one day he would return from the Golden Mountain to finish the Work and drive out the Manchus. When he did, Father and Mother and I would be right by his side" (page 7)

_____
_____
_____
_____

Create new pages and add to this list as you read the rest of the book.

Reasons for Immigration

One of the novel's key themes is immigration and what drives people to leave their homeland for a strange, new place. Here are some important questions to consider while reading this novel.

- What entices people to give up all they have to move somewhere else?

- Why are people willing to leave friends and family?

- What conditions at home force or encourage people to leave their homelands?

- Why are people willing to take such risks?

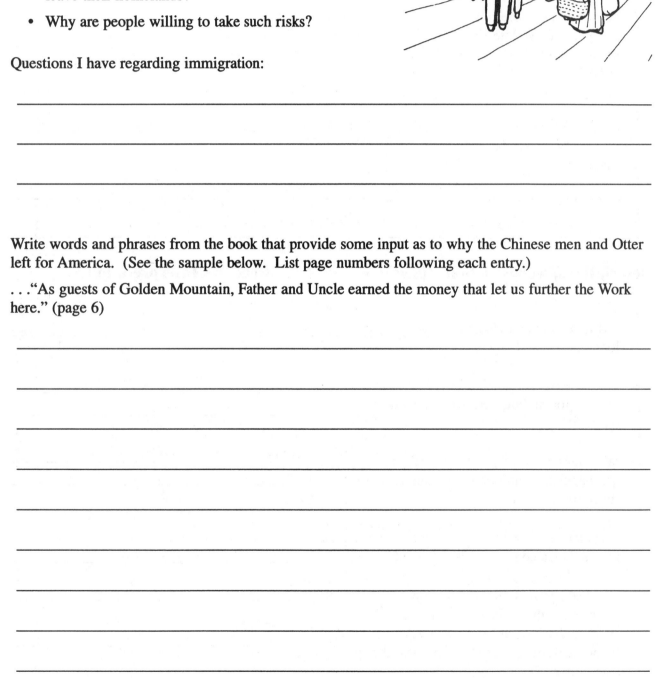

Questions I have regarding immigration:

_____

_____

_____

Write words and phrases from the book that provide some input as to why the Chinese men and Otter left for America. (See the sample below. List page numbers following each entry.)

. . ."As guests of Golden Mountain, Father and Uncle earned the money that let us further the Work here." (page 6)

_____

_____

_____

_____

_____

_____

_____

Reader's Response Journal

Writing can help clarify thinking. It is an active process that requires students to put their thoughts, feelings, and ideas into words. To build greater meaning and personal understanding of *Dragon's Gate*, have students create their own reader's response journals. Requiring journals of your students ensures that all students make a response to what they are reading. A reader's response journal provides students with a written record of their thoughts as they progress through the book. It encourages the students to go back and reread passages of the novel and to reflect upon what they are reading. Reader's response journals also help students become personally involved in the book as they react to the characters' conflicts, actions, and words.

Here are some ideas for using reader's response journals in your classroom:

- **Discuss the purpose** of reader's response journals. Motivate the class by encouraging the students to use their journals as a way to express their personal feelings about the book and related issues in their own lives.

- **Provide mini-notebooks** or assemble journals. To make journals, you can use one piece of 12" x 18" (30 cm x 46 cm) construction paper, several sheets of notebook paper, and three paper fasteners to form a booklet. Students can create a cover design and make their journal notes inside.

- Using passages from the book, **model the journal process**. Show students how you would record your own feelings, thoughts, ideas, observations, and questions about what you have read. Then do a few passages together as a class.

- Provide students with **journal starters** such as these:

I noticed that the character . . .	This reminds me of . . .
It's hard for me to imagine . . .	I've felt that way when . . .
If this happened to me, I would . . .	I don't understand why . . .
I'm confused about . . .	In this chapter, I learned . . .

- **Keep a chart with new journal response starters** that the students create.

- **Provide passages** from the book to which students may respond. Then have students choose passages they feel compelled to respond to.

Here are some examples from Section One:

—"The Golden Mountain, it seemed, was now only a poetical metaphor."

—"You can't let other people live your life for you."

—"Be careful what you wish, for it may come true."

- Have volunteers **share their responses**. Provide feedback to the students, acknowledging their responses and encouraging greater clarity when needed.

(**Note to the teacher:** Due to the complexity of the story, teachers may want students to read and answer chapters 7-9 questions after reading that part of the book and save the remaining questions until chapters 10–12 have been read. Have students write responses on separate paper.)

Quiz Time

Chapters 7–9

1. Describe the voyage to America. (How long? Conditions? Risks? etc.)

2. What observations does Otter make about the land and the way it had been used?

3. What advantages did Otter have over the others?

4. List all the details you can that show how unprepared (or unaware) the immigrants were for what they had to face. Include things that relate to differences in culture. You may include details from chapter 7.

5. What can you learn about Sean's dad by what Sean says on the sledge trip?

6. Reread the descriptions on pages 70 and 71. To what is the mountain being compared? How does that description add to the tension in the story?

7. What does Otter expect when he uses what he calls the "magic name Foxfire"?

8. Describe Father's reaction to having his son with him on the mountain. What lets you know that Otter has made a terrible mistake?

Chapters 10–12

9. Otter meets Foxfire in America for the first time. In what ways does Foxfire seem different to Otter from the person he was in China? What do you think causes this change?

10. Why did the westerners call all the Chinese "John"? How do you think that made them feel?

11. Otter says Foxfire lied about America. Foxfire defends himself by saying he told only half the truth. Is there a difference between the two? Is one more "right" than the other? Explain your answer.

12. Reread page 94. Foxfire explains that the Americans are better in theory than in practice. What was he trying to explain?

13. Describe the treatment of the Chinese. What are their working and living conditions? How are they viewed by the westerners? Provide specific details from chapters 7–12 to support your ideas.

14. From what you have read in chapters 7–12, what evidence do you have that this railroad will be built no matter the risk or the cost to land and people?

15. Why do the other Chinese workers make fun of Otter?

Create a Picture Postcard

Otter has left his homeland and his way of life. He lost his status and almost everything he knows. Now in this dehumanizing setting, Otter must meet the challenges of his new life in America. So much of what he envisioned and was promised is a myth.

Pretend you are Otter. For this activity, you will write a postcard letter to someone at home. Tell your mother or a friend about the new life you are facing. Be specific in your details, so another villager does not make the same mistake as you. You may use ideas from Section One. Make sure your words sound like those Otter would use.

Then use a 5" x 8" (13 cm x 20 cm) index card, construction paper, or the boxes below to create your picture postcard. On the front of the card, draw a picture which clearly shows where you are now in America. On the back, write your letter.

Front

Draw your picture in this box.

Back

Have your postmark fit the time period and where you are in America. Design a stamp that might have been used at that time. Create an address for the person in China to whom you are sending this card. Write your letter in the space provided.

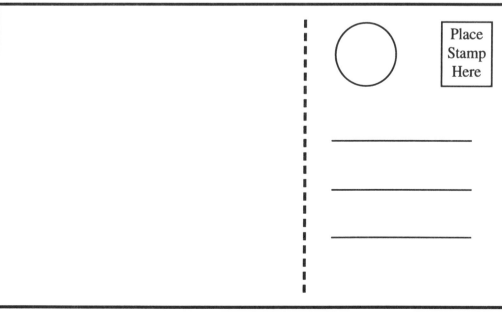

Culture Clues

Throughout *Dragon's Gate*, we get a glimpse of Chinese culture. To understand another culture, we have to become aware of what the people believe and how and why they behave the way they do. We also need to understand the traditions and circumstances that have shaped their lives.

Culture is formed by language, religion, government, ancestry, and the ways a group of people live their lives. Traditions, ceremonies, celebrations, and beliefs are all a part of a group's culture.

With your teacher's help, form cooperative groups. In your group, divide up the chapters you have read thus far so that each group member has a section of the book for which he or she is responsible. Group members are to reread their sections. Use the space below to jot down anything that seems to reflect the Chinese culture.

Example: "The astrologers say you were born in the hour of the fire, in the month of fire, so you were bound to join my family, because we've been rebels and troublemakers for seven generations." (page 5)

When everyone has finished, group members can share the findings with each other, and discuss what the examples mean. Then your group can share the "culture clues" you found with the entire class.

_____

_____

_____

_____

_____

_____

_____

_____

_____

_____

_____

_____

Status

Throughout the novel, concerns about status, position, and power are intertwined. What is status? How do people attain it or achieve it? How do people lose the status they once had?

What is status?

Status refers to the social standing one has as viewed by others. It is related to the position or rank one has in a group. It is the prestige that someone has that often determines whether or not he or she has power in a group.

What determines status?

Status is determined by the structure of the social or cultural group. In some cultures, older people have greater status than younger people, while in some cultures the elders receive far less respect and prestige. In some groups, status is something you obtain at birth based on sex, race, religion, and/or your family's financial history and occupations.

Status can also be earned or achieved. When someone succeeds in his or her particular field, greater status or prestige is attributed to that individual.

How is status viewed in the novel?

Look below at the passages from the novel. (*Italics* refer to the English dialogue being spoken in the book.) Using these questions, discuss each one and analyze what the passage says about status:

- What is the Chinese view of status?

- What is the American view?

- What issues does Otter have regarding status? Why does he hide the fact that he is born a Stranger?

- Does status change? Why?

- How was the status obtained — was it earned or ascribed?

- How does status relate to stereotypes? Prejudice? Discrimination?

Passages:

1. "There were two groups of boys in our school: those whose fathers had stayed here and those whose fathers had gone overseas to *America*. . . . The difference was often between the poor and the rich. Since the guests paid for the school, their sons led a privileged life. The other boys, though, were fair game." (page 3)

2. "What do you do when your family is so powerful that you lead a charmed life and even your teacher won't find fault with you?" (page 3)

3. "All my life I had been taught that if you're born poor or even a slave, you must have done something bad in your previous life." (page 33)

Status *(cont.)*

——————— How is status viewed in the novel? *(cont.)* ———————

Passages (cont.):

4. *"Everybody there, they free. Everybody, they equal."* (In America) (page 33)

5. "Our name has clout with the agents." (page 51)

6. "In Three Willows, the poorer boys and I could be familiar with one another; but a look or a certain tone were enough to remind them of their place." (page 56)

7. "You're awfully tall. Tall enough to be a Stranger. We cut most of your kind down to size." (page 56)

8. "What status did I have with the westerners now?" (page 67)

9. "I reluctantly decided that I wasn't going to get any help unless I used the magic name . . .

   'Just give us directions to my Uncle Foxfire and we'll leave.' " (page 76)

10. "Could he be as much of an outcast among his own kind as I was?" (page 121)

———————— How does status affect my life? ————————

• What does our society value and respect in its people?

• Who seems to have the most status?

• Do you think we should view status based on what someone acquires at birth, or should we view status based on what someone accomplishes?

• What influences our view of status and prestige?

• What effect do advertising and the media have on our views?

• What are status symbols? Why are they important to people? Do you think status should be placed on the material things a person owns or what a person accomplishes?

———————— Reflecting on the Learning ————————

Use your reader's response journal to answer the following questions:

• What is status?

• What did you learn from this discussion?

• How does status affect your life?

• What else can you share about this topic?

Look for places in the book that relate to status as you continue your reading. Think about the issues you have discussed today. See whether you can expand your understanding of status.

Express Yourself

Literature is a vehicle for us to learn not only about others, but also about ourselves. An author's words create vivid mental images and tap into our own experiences. The struggles a character endures or difficulties a character conquers can illuminate familiar themes in our own lives.

Writing can open the doors of our hearts and minds for reflection and self-growth. Read each of the following writing prompts. Decide which one best relates to you. Once you have made your choice, reread the prompt and reflect upon what you want to share about yourself. On separate paper, brainstorm the ideas that you might include in your writing. Then, when you think you have organized your thoughts, express them on paper. See what you learn about yourself in the process.

Choice #1: "Let Me Grow Up"

Remember a time when you really wanted to do something on your own, but your parents felt you were not old enough yet. You finally got the chance to do what you wanted, and the reality of your independence sank in. How did doing this activity feel? How did you feel about being on your own? What was exciting about it? What turned out to be scary?

In your writing, tell what it is you longed to do on your own. Explain why your parents wanted you to wait and why they finally allowed you to have your way. Tell how your new independence felt and what was positive and negative about doing the particular thing you wanted. Take time to make your thoughts and feelings clear.

Choice #2: "I Did Not Know It Would Be Like This"

When Otter finally got his wish to go to America, he realized that getting what you want is not always what you expect. Think of a time when you could have used Otter's same words, "I did not know it was going to be like this." It can be a time when things were much worse than you expected or when things actually were much better than expected.

In your writing, describe clearly what the situation was. Tell what you expected and how and why things were so much different from your expectations. Finally, tell what you learned from this experience.

(**Note to the teacher:** Due to the complexity of the story, teachers may want students to read and answer chapters 13–15 questions after reading that part of the book and save the remaining questions until chapters 16–18 have been read. Have students write responses on separate paper.)

Quiz Time

Chapters 13–15

1. What experience described in Chapter 13 is so humiliating for Otter? Why do Foxfire and Father let the experience occur?

2. Three rules of survival are also mentioned: Keep warm, keep dry, and keep clean. Tell why these rules are important. Why do the cabin men insist that Otter follow these rules?

3. Sean expresses that most of the time living on Tiger Mountain is actually better than being at home. Tell about Sean's childhood and why life on the mountain seems better to him.

4. Why does Otter feel that his home village is really not his home?

5. Otter and Sean come from different worlds, and yet they are becoming friends. What brings them together as friends? Describe many details from their pasts and their lives on the mountain that reveal the growing bond between them.

6. One reaction Sean has to both the deaths of Shifty and his mother is that those who have died are far better off than he. Why does Sean feel this way?

7. When Sean and Otter shared a meal together, it created anger among many. Who was angry and why?

8. "It didn't matter where we were from or who we had once been. On the mountain, he and I were in a secret conspiracy against the world." (page 132) Explain what this quote means.

9. Why does Kilroy encourage one of the big men to fight his son? How does Kilroy react to the outcome?

10. Reread pages 140 and 141. Why is the railroad important to Kilroy? How are his dreams similar to Uncle Foxfire's?

Chapters 16–18

11. What happens to Doggy's moon guitar? Why are the cabin mates so saddened by its loss?

12. What does Otter do that finally wins him the approval of his cabin mates? Why are these men proud of Otter?

13. What great tragedy comes to Doggy? Why is his loss felt by all his cabin mates?

14. What positive outcome comes out of Doggy's tragedy? Why do you think this happened?

15. Explain how Otter's anger helps him learn how to drive the pickax at the mountain.

16. Otter cannot find his father after the explosion. Why do the men have to leave Father behind? What do you think will happen to Father?

"Just how do you eat with those things anyway?"

A conversation between Sean and Otter about chopsticks illustrates a cultural difference in eating between the Chinese and the Americans. Later in the conversation, Sean is surprised that Otter can get the food to his mouth with the chopsticks, while Otter is surprised that Sean does not stab himself with the fork.

With your class, discuss various cultural eating styles that people have experienced in their own families or while traveling. While being respectful of the differences, share unusual foods, mannerisms, ways of sitting, etc.

Ask a local Chinese restaurant if they would donate a class set of chopsticks. Make the Chinese rice dish below and try eating Chinese style.

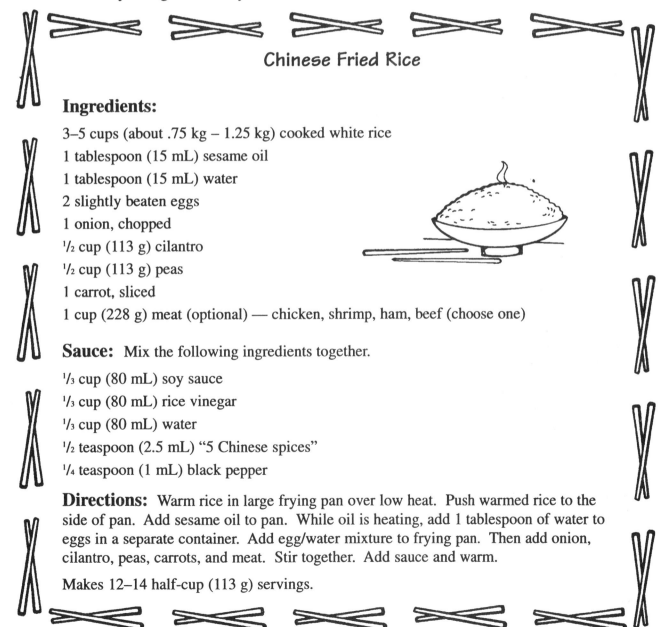

Chinese Fried Rice

Ingredients:

3–5 cups (about .75 kg – 1.25 kg) cooked white rice

1 tablespoon (15 mL) sesame oil

1 tablespoon (15 mL) water

2 slightly beaten eggs

1 onion, chopped

½ cup (113 g) cilantro

½ cup (113 g) peas

1 carrot, sliced

1 cup (228 g) meat (optional) — chicken, shrimp, ham, beef (choose one)

Sauce: Mix the following ingredients together.

⅓ cup (80 mL) soy sauce

⅓ cup (80 mL) rice vinegar

⅓ cup (80 mL) water

½ teaspoon (2.5 mL) "5 Chinese spices"

¼ teaspoon (1 mL) black pepper

Directions: Warm rice in large frying pan over low heat. Push warmed rice to the side of pan. Add sesame oil to pan. While oil is heating, add 1 tablespoon of water to eggs in a separate container. Add egg/water mixture to frying pan. Then add onion, cilantro, peas, carrots, and meat. Stir together. Add sauce and warm.

Makes 12–14 half-cup (113 g) servings.

Home Sweet Home

The Chinese men who worked on Tiger Mountain lived in incredibly crowded living quarters. To truly get a sense of what their living conditions were like, try one or more of the following projects. You may come up with some of your own ideas, too.

Use the following definitions to help you with these projects.

> **Scale:** Use a standard measure to determine size; a scale drawing would be drawn to the exact proportions of the real thing.
>
> **Show, Not Tell:** This is a technique in writing where the author uses description to "paint" a mind picture for the reader. The author "shows" the reader by writing specific details to create the image, rather than simply "telling" the reader.

Sidewalk Chalk Cabin Models — Group Project

1. Reread pages 115 (bottom) to 116. Notice how the author's "show, not tell" descriptions paint a clear picture in the reader's mind about the cabin in which the men lived.

2. In note form, jot down specific details about the cabin: its size, contents, what it is made of, etc.

3. Using sidewalk chalk, go outside and draw the actual dimensions (scale would match the measurements given in the book) of the cabin and the bunks. In the space remaining, draw in where the stove and other items in the cabin would have to fit.

Log Cabin Models — Group Project

1. Reread pages 115 (bottom) to 116. Notice how the author's "show, not tell" descriptions paint a clear picture in the readers' minds about the cabin in which the men lived.

2. In note form, jot down specific details about the cabin: its size, contents, what it is made of, etc.

3. Using wood twigs, craft sticks, or Lincoln Logs, construct a log cabin model to scale. (The model would be smaller, but still have the same proportions as the dimensions provided in the book. This would be a scale model of the real thing.) Use details from the book to complete your model. For instance, add newspaper strips to fill in the cracks between the logs. Make bunkbeds in the tier formation described in the book.

Scale Drawings — Floor Plan — Partner Project

1. Follow steps 1 and 2 above.

2. Using graph paper, make a scale drawing floor plan of the cabin and bunks. Add other details from the book to show what was inside these cabins.

Reflecting on the Learning — On Your Own

When you have finished the above projects, write a paragraph or two about how you would feel living with so many people in such a small space. Remember, too, that these cabins lacked electricity, plumbing, and other conveniences that we have today.

Don't Take Me Literally

Many expressions that Laurence Yep uses are examples of figurative language or idioms. These phrases have great meaning, but do not translate literally word for word. See if you can determine the meaning of Laurence Yep's words from *Dragon's Gate.*

> **Directions:** Read each of the statements below. Locate the sentence in the book. Use the context of the words to help you determine what the expression means. Write the statement's meaning in the blank provided.

1. "In the back of my mind. . . " (page 48)

   _____

2. ". . . things are either black or white, and there's no such color as gray." (page 114)

   _____

3. ". . . you can't set the world on fire right away." (page 115)

   _____

4. "I've got a good mind to go anyway." (page 117)

   _____

5. ". . . there was a twinkle in his eye. . . " (page 117)

   _____

6. "Doggy tickles the strings." (page 117)

   _____

7. "It's about time you started pulling your own weight." (page 126)

   _____

8. "Let's see if you got any sand." (page 135)

   _____

9. "You're yellow — just like the Chinamen you love. . . " (page 135)

   _____

10. "Except squeeze you into a bottle?" (page 141)

    _____

Now see if you can find some of your own!

The Strength of the Human Spirit

Life on the mountain was much worse than Otter ever expected, and yet he finds that his fellow Chinese men have found ways to deal with their anguish. Father described the simple hobbies that all the cabin mates have. Bright Star learned to carve from Shaky, and Noodles did a little painting. Doggy "tickled the strings," Father was "snipping," and Packy traded for things he and his cabin mates needed.

Have you ever wondered if you could handle some of the great hardships other people must endure? Consider the following questions: How do people survive great hardships and suffering? How does a hobby help someone deal with stress? What physical activities do people do to relieve their anger and/or stress? What are some positive ways you deal with stress?

Interview: How did you cope?

Conduct an interview to learn more about the strength of the human spirit. Think of someone you know who has endured some terrible hardship. Perhaps you know someone who has lost a loved one. Maybe you know a friend, a relative, or a famous person who endured a painful illness, injury, or medical treatment. How did these people survive their experiences? What did this person do with his or her hands or their minds to make it through the suffering? Discuss with your teacher and/or parent if they feel it would be appropriate to interview this person about his/her experience. On a piece of paper, write several interview questions you might ask this person or use the questions below.

Sample Interview Questions

Name of Interviewee:_____

Hardship Experienced: _____

- What was most difficult about your experience? When did it happen?
- Have you recovered from the pain?
- What did you do to help yourself cope?
- What, if any, hobbies or activities did you do to take your mind off the pain and suffering?
- What people helped you through your hard times?
- What advice do you have for others who might be experiencing the same loss or pain?
- In what ways did you grow from the experience?
- What would you like others to know about what you have been through?

(**Note to the teacher:** Due to the complexity of the story, teachers may want students to read and answer chapters 19–21 questions after reading that part of the book, and save the remaining questions until chapters 23–24 have been read. Have students write responses on separate paper.)

Quiz Time

Chapters 19–21

1. Explain the following quote: "It was all very well for dreamers to have dreams; but the rest of us got hurt, too." (page 168)

2. What is Kilroy's reaction to the explosion? What does he expect the men to do afterwards?

3. Why do you think Kilroy feels he has to use his whip on Otter? Do you think he is justified in doing so?

4. What does Foxfire mean when he says, "Anger is a luxury up here." (page 179)

5. How does Father cope with his blindness?

6. Why does Otter treat his cabin mates and Sean so bitterly after the whipping?

7. "When the crew got off their shift, they came into the cabin as if they were going to a funeral." Why is the crew feeling this way? (page 181)

Chapters 22–24

8. Why do the Chinese men lack the power to stand up to their American bosses when the Chinese outnumber the Americans?

9. Reread Otter's dream on page 183. Interpret its meaning.

10. Why do you think the other crews mock Otter after the whipping?

11. Uncle Foxfire loses his support from the crew. All the men desert him when he is arguing with Kilroy. Why do the men walk away? For what is Foxfire fighting?

12. In chapter 23, Otter begins to see Foxfire in a new light. What are the many things he realizes about Foxfire?

13. What does Foxfire do to show that he wants to keep his promise to return Otter home safely?

14. What changes do you see in Otter from when he was in China?

15. Why do you think Sean decides to go with Otter and Foxfire to set the explosives when it is something he does not have to do?

"I'm Blind"

Those were the words spoken by Father when he finally realized that had he lost his sight. Imagine how frightening it would be to experience sudden blindness. Think about all the things you would have to relearn to do. Think of the things you would never be able to do without assistance.

Try these activities to help you understand the role sight plays in your life. You may also create your own activities to explore blindness. See how very simple tasks become much more difficult. The gift of sight is one that most of us take for granted.

Materials:

- blindfolds (15 or more)
- collection of clothing, large enough for children to put over their clothes
- shoes to be laced
- geoboards with rubber bands
- crayons and paper

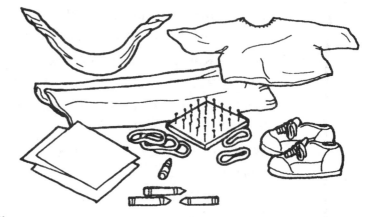

Directions:

1. Set up centers around the room. You will need two clothing stations, two shoe stations, and two geoboard stations.

2. Place crayons and paper on students' desks.

3. Have students rotate through the stations in small groups, trying on clothing, lacing shoes, and using rubber bands to make geoboard designs while blindfolded.

4. As students await their turns, have them draw something with the crayons and papers at their desks. Have them do one side of the paper with their eyes open and the other side of the paper with their eyes closed.

Follow-up Discussion:

1. Have you ever had the experience of not being able to see well in a new place or being somewhere strange where you had to walk alone in the dark? Describe how it felt.

2. Describe how these simple jobs were changed when you could not see what you were doing.

3. What did you do to compensate for your temporary loss of sight?

4. What would you have to do differently to learn things at school?

5. Describe how it would feel if you had to have someone else help you do things that other people can do alone.

6. How can you be more sensitive to others who need help doing things that are simple for you?

Beyond "Once upon a Time"

While many fairy tales begin with "Once upon a time," most authors use the first line of a story to set the tone and engage the reader's interest. Good last lines of books work to leave the reader feeling a sense of closure and inspire the reader to reflect upon the book.

Talented authors like Laurence Yep choose their titles carefully to make a connection between the title and the text. Mr. Yep pulls the reader into the book with exciting action in the very first line and provides food for thought with his final words. The following activity will make you aware of titles, first lines, and last lines and how they help you focus on what the author feels is important about his or her story. It can also help you be a better writer, encouraging you to create words that grab your readers and keep them interested.

Materials:

- collection of favorite books (Have each member of your group bring in one book for this lesson.)
- construction paper, butcher paper, or sentence strips
- marking pens

Directions:

1. With your class, read and discuss the first line, last line, and title of *Dragon's Gate*. How did the author use his first line to entice you to read more? Since you have not finished the book, what do you think of the last line? How does it make you feel? What importance does the title have to the story? Why do you think the author chose *Dragon's Gate* to be the title?

2. In your small groups, each member should share his or her favorite book. While sharing, read the first line, last line, and the title of the book, and tell why this is your favorite book.

3. After everyone in the group has shared, the group members should select their favorite first line, last line, and title among the books. These do not have to be from the same book. On the construction, butcher, or sentence-strip paper, copy the favorite first line, last line, and title separately.

4. Assemble all the first lines, last lines, and titles in groupings on the board where everyone can see them. Have a group member share your group's choices.

5. Conclude this activity with a class discussion, the following questions: What do these first lines have in common? Are there some that stick out in some way? What is unusual about them? How do they catch the reader's interest? What do you like about them? (Repeat the discussion for the last lines.) What makes a book title interesting? What significance does the book title have to the rest of the book?

Extra! Extra! Read All About It!

An avalanche has sent a death trap of snow rolling onto the mountain, smothering cabins and trapping many workers. The threat of another avalanche looms as the falling snow builds upon the mountain.

Pretend you are a newspaper reporter who has been sent up to the mountain to report this latest event. Dig up the important facts and list them in the five W's below. Think of an eye-catching headline. Then, write your news story below.

Who: _____

What: _____

Where: _____

When: _____

Why: _____

_____
Headline

_____

_____

_____

_____

_____

_____

_____

Dreams

In section four, dreams are mentioned several times. Foxfire was referred to as a dreamer, but he was also blamed for his dreams hurting others. Otter had a powerful dream that stirred many emotions and gave him ideas to ponder. Those ideas affected the decisions he later made.

In this assignment, you will explore these two aspects of dreams — your dreams. In the first part you will think and write about your wishes and dreams for the future. Try to share only those things that you are willing to work hard to achieve. In the second part, recall a nighttime dream that gave you food for thought. Tell what happened in the dream and what importance it had (or has) for you.

My Hopes and Dreams for the Future

One night I dreamed . . .

(**Note to the teacher:** Due to the complexity of the story, teachers may want students to read and answer chapters 25–27 questions after reading that part of the book and save the remaining questions until chapters 28–30 have been read. Have students write responses on separate paper.)

Quiz Time

Chapters 25–27

1. Foxfire is not the man Otter thought he was. However, in what ways is Foxfire still a hero?

2. Reread page 39 and page 217 where Otter talks about Dragon's Gate. What is he telling himself about life in discussing the tradition of Dragon's Gate?

3. Explain the following quote by Foxfire, "There's no magic. It's what's inside you."

4. Being alone on the mountain peak, Foxfire and Otter reexamine their lives and dreams. What discoveries have they made about life and each other?

5. In what ways did the author foreshadow (give hints) that Foxfire was going to die?

6. Provide evidence to show that Otter gained the respect of the workers.

7. What responsibilities does Otter feel he has to fulfill before he can go home?

Chapters 28–30

8. Why do you think Otter and the men finally had the courage to stand up to Kilroy and walk off the job after Kilroy asked Doggy to stop singing?

9. What do you see happening to Otter's personality as he leads the men in standing up to Kilroy?

10. Why does the pay raise deepen the men's anger rather than make them happy?

11. Interpret Otter's dream (pages 261–262). What message does it have for him?

12. What gives people the strength and determination to strike when they risk losing their jobs, their wages, or being punished?

13. Why does Otter give up his search for Foxfire's bones when it is such an important cultural tradition? How does his decision show that Otter is becoming more like Foxfire?

14. Explain the following quote from page 270: "They can have their little ceremony. We know the truth."

15. From reading the Afterword, what can you tell about the work a writer must do in order to write a historical novel?

My Box of Treasures

After Foxfire's death, Otter gathers Foxfire's belongings so he can ship them home. Among his possessions, Otter finds a small basket. In it are belongings more precious than Foxfire's mansion and gardens back home in China. Otter describes the contents on page 236. ("Despite his mansion and gardens back at home . . .")

Think of all the things you own. What are some of your most treasured possessions? What are some of the little pieces of "trash or junk" that you continue to keep? Do you still have ticket stubs to a special play or sports event? Do you have a lock of your baby hair? What are the things you have outgrown or no longer need but you still have?

The following project will help you to learn about yourself and to share yourself with others:

1. Assemble a box or basket of some of your sacred treasures. They can be things of worldly value, or junk/trash-like items that you still want to keep. You might want to decorate your box, or find something special in which to put your items.

2. On separate index cards, write what each item is, and why it is special to you. Tell what you think these items say about you as a person.

3. Prepare an oral presentation about your box. Share your treasures with the class. Think about what you have learned about yourself in gathering your prized possessions.

Here is a rubric that your teacher might use to grade your project:

Name _____ **Date** _____

Content:

Treasures (5 items, minimum) _____ 5 pts. _____

Index cards describing each item _____ 5 pts. _____

Oral Presentation:

Eye contact _____ 2 pts. _____

Able to be heard _____ 2 pts. _____

Poised _____ 2 pts. _____

Total Points _____ 16 pts. _____

Looking at the Story Line

Key elements of literature are combined to put together a good book. The story line is the path the story follows with the key elements woven through it. In this activity, you will work in groups to find these elements and see how they come together to form the novel's story line. You will find that Laurence Yep carefully planned his story so that all the pieces fit together perfectly.

Definitions

(The following definitions are expressed in terms appropriate for the lesson.)

Setting: where and when the story takes place

Characters: the people (or animals) who are involved in the story

    Protagonist: the main character

    Antagonist: a character who is in conflict with the main character; an opponent

Problem: the obstacle(s) or conflict(s) that the main character must solve or overcome

Resolution/Solution: how the problem is resolved

Rising Action: the events that build the story

Climax: the point where the conflict is at its peak; where resolution is in sight, but the outcome is not yet certain

Falling Action: the events that follow the climax and bring the story to closure

Theme: the message about life that a reader may learn from the story

Directions:

1. Divide the class into the following groups. Group One will gather information on the setting(s). They should gather descriptions that make the setting vivid. They might want to illustrate the settings. Group Two will do the characters, including protagonist and antagonist. They should provide descriptions of the characters' personalities and physical appearances. Group Three will do the problem and resolution/solution, and groups Four, Five, and Six will all do the rising action, climax, and the falling action.

2. Each group will search the book and gather information for their topic. They will find a way to present their information to the class, either in words or in pictures. The groups involved with the rising and falling action events may want to brainstorm the key events first and then meet with the other groups doing the same and come to consensus on what is the climax. The falling action will be easier to accomplish.

3. Each group can present their piece. The class can discuss the information, and students may suggest additions or deletions. Finally, the students may discuss the theme and how all the pieces fit together to make a developed story line.

Words with Multiple Meanings

Laurence Yep writes his novels with great command of the English language. His word choice and usage create precise meanings and images in his work.

Some words have many meanings. Mr. Yep sometimes chooses the less common meanings of words. The only way to discover the correct definition of a multiple meaning word is in the context of its sentence. For example, a bat is an animal, and it is also a piece of baseball equipment. You know which meaning is meant by the way the word is used in the sentence: The bat cracked when she hit the home run.

Directions: Read the sets of sentences. Identify the word from the list below that should be used in each set. Then, on the lines provided, write definitions for each use of the word.

Word List

mess	flounder	relish	strike
subscription	resort	agent	

---

1. Please pass the _____ so I can put it on my hot dog. He did not _____ this meal as much as the last year's feast.

    a. _____

    b. _____

2. Did you renew your magazine ___? Most of the ___ from his new school was paid for by his grandfather.

    a. _____

    b. _____

3. A chemical ___ was used in the mixture. The government ___ will arrange passage for me to travel to America.

    a. _____

    b. _____

4. This bedroom is a terrible ___ . Will you be eating in the ___ hall?

    a. _____

    b. _____

5. I caught a ___ on my vacation. When Otter became cold, he began to ___ in the snow.

    a. _____

    b. _____

6. Will you go on ___ to demand more wages? I will ___ the ball.

    a. _____

    b. _____

7. Will you be staying at the Hawaiian ___? I did not want to ___ to using violence to get my way.

    a. _____

    b. _____

Take a Stand!

Throughout history, people have taken a stand for what they believe in order to make the world a better place. Sometimes that requires great risk — either physically risking one's life, or emotionally risking the respect and approval of others. Otter risked his life and the respect of his cabin mates by taking a stand against Kilroy's harsh ways.

Class Discussion

Discuss the instances in the novel where someone took a stand.

- What was the issue?
- What was at risk?
- What was the final outcome?
- What consequences did the person suffer?
- Were the results worth the risks?

Discuss other issues today or in history where people have taken a stand. Use the questions above to discuss these issues.

- Why is it important to consider the possible consequences before taking an action?
- What are some ways you can take a stand? What are the possible outcomes and consequences for those actions? What ways might work best for you? Why?

Activity

Choose one of the issues below or pick one of your own. Think of a way to make your opinion known. It can be one of the ways discussed above, or it can be in the form of a letter to the editor of a newspaper, a poster, a speech, or an argument for a debate.

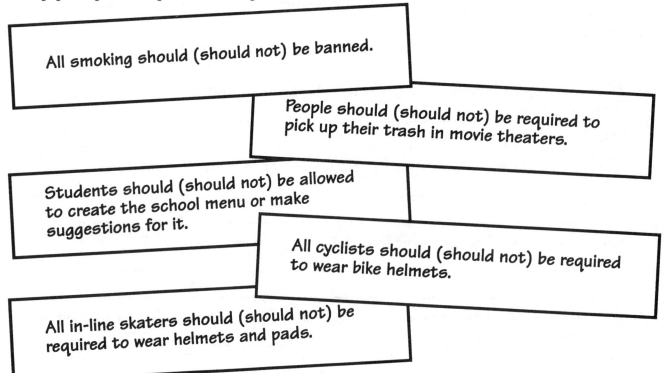

All smoking should (should not) be banned.

People should (should not) be required to pick up their trash in movie theaters.

Students should (should not) be allowed to create the school menu or make suggestions for it.

All cyclists should (should not) be required to wear bike helmets.

All in-line skaters should (should not) be required to wear helmets and pads.

Book Report Ideas

Share the power and excitement of *Dragon's Gate* by choosing one or more of the following activities. You will be amazed at how much you have learned by reading this captivating novel.

- **Book Blurb**

  Look at the backs of several paperback books. Notice how the publisher has provided an enticing summary of the book, without giving away any of the important details. Write your own "book blurb" about *Dragon's Gate*. Choose words that will grab your readers and make them want to read this book. Be careful to give hints about the dangers of the mountain and the experiences Otter faced, without spoiling the story for them. These book blurbs could be saved in a class book with other blurbs created throughout the year. Then, the book could be used as a reference file for choosing good literature.

- **Picture/Quote Book**

  You will be assigned one chapter of the book. Reread the chapter to determine the most important scenes, events, or conversations from the chapter. Illustrate a scene on 8 ½" x 11" (22 cm x 28 cm) construction paper or plain paper. Then, choose a few sentences from the book that best describe the scene and write them at the bottom of the picture. Your picture will be added to others to make a class book.

- **Add a Chapter**

  The railroad is finished, and Otter has survived his ordeal. What will he do now? Continue Otter's story.

- **TV Talk Show**

  For this activity, your classroom needs to be set up like a talk show studio. Choose a host. Your classmates will be celebrity guests on the show. These guests represent the various characters in the book. Have the host conduct interviews and take questions from the audience.

- **Diorama**

  Construct the mountain, its tunnels, cabins, and surroundings as you picture it. Create a diorama or some type of three-dimensional display of the setting.

- **Mini Museum**

  Bring in or make items mentioned in the book (pickaxes, chopsticks, etc.). Set up a table of artifacts. Make a label and write a description for each item. Then, invite another class to visit the "museum" to learn about the book.

- **Time Line**

  Using details from the story, create a possible time line for the book. Write major events of the story on the time line. A date, a caption, and a picture should mark each event.

- **Life-Sized Charts**

  Trace the outlines of the students' bodies on butcher paper. Have students create a life-sized picture of Otter. On the body have them write in various character traits he possessed: physical, moral, emotional, social, etc. Students could also do these for Kilroy, Foxfire, Mother, Father, and Sean. The charts can be done in teams, and a bulletin board can be created with these figures.

Research Ideas

In your reading you got a taste of many fascinating topics, such as building the transcontinental railroad, Chinese immigration, blindness, avalanches, and explosives. Think about what interested you most and what you would like to learn and research in more depth.

Write three questions you would like answered. (Examples: What causes avalanches? Can they be controlled and/or prevented? How can someone out in the snow avoid being harmed by an avalanche?)

My questions:

1._____

2._____

3._____

Work in groups or alone to research at least one of the questions you wrote above. You can also choose from one of the topics listed below. Share what you have learned with the class. Create a chart, draw diagrams, write a description, or make an oral presentation with your findings.

- Transcontinental railroad
- Chinese immigration
- Avalanches
- Explosives used to build tunnels, railroads, etc.
- Survival in the mountains
- Chinese cooking
- Manchus
- Dragons
- History of China
- The Opium Wars
- Drug addiction
- Effects of the transcontinental railroad on Native Americans
- Positive outcomes of the transcontinental railroad
- Steam locomotives
- Theodore Judah — promoter of the transcontinental railroad
- The Great Race — the Union Pacific and Central Pacific Companies
- The Big Four — businessmen who invested in the railroad
- Irish workers on the railroad
- Popular railroad songs
- Chinese language
- Blindness

I've Changed

The point of reading literature is to gain insight about life as a process for change. What makes a story compelling is exploring that process through its characters. The more an author can have us empathize and relate to a character, the more connected we feel with the writing. In addition, through the exploration of a character's change and growth, we can often learn about our own process of change.

Class Discussion

Look back at the changes Otter experienced. Share your thoughts about the following questions:

- What events in Otter's life have shaped his life?
- What key experiences have encouraged Otter to examine who he is?
- In what ways has Otter grown and changed from his days in China to the day the final spike of the transcontinental railroad was driven?
- What has Otter learned about himself and others?
- What has Otter learned about life?

Activities

1. **Character Venn Diagram**

   While discussing the questions above, complete the following Venn diagram. In the left circle, record what Otter was like in the beginning. Then, look at how he has changed by the end of the book and record those changes in the right circle. In the middle, add the details that show the ways he has remained the same.

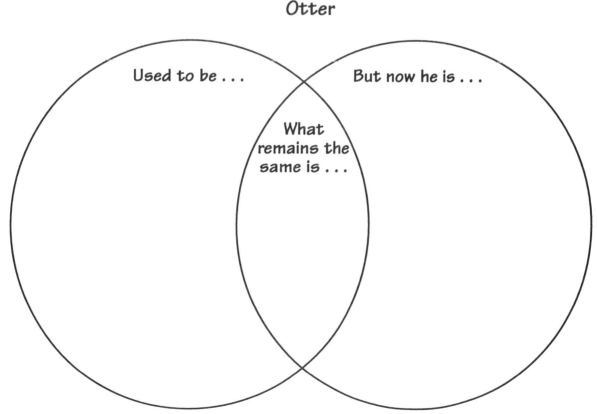

Otter

Used to be . . .   What remains the same is . . .   But now he is . . .

I've Changed (cont.)

═══════════════════════ **Activities** (cont.) ═══════════════════════

2. Personal Exploration

Think about your life and how you have changed.

- What events have shaped your life? (a move, parents' divorce, new sibling, illness, awards, etc.)
- What key experiences have encouraged you to examine who you are?
- In what ways have you changed and grown? (fears you have overcome, things you can do, etc.)
- What have you learned about yourself?
- What would you like others to know about you?

3. Personal Venn Diagram — Prewriting Activity

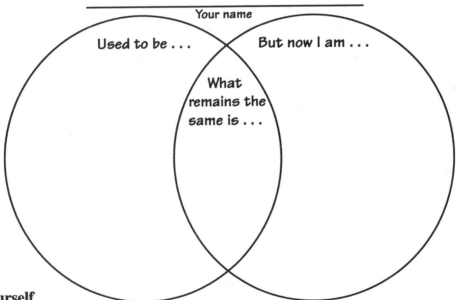

Your name

Used to be . . .

But now I am . . .

What remains the same is . . .

4. Express Yourself

Are there things about yourself you wish for others to know about you? Have you changed in ways that you wish others would see? Using the insights you have gained from the above activities, express yourself and let others know who you are. Think about the best way to accomplish this. Write a song, a poem, or story, or create some visual presentation. You may paint a picture or create a collage. This is your chance to tell the world who you are. Use your creative juices and let them flow into some finished piece.

Now, express yourself in a poem that will allow you to share a bit of yourself with others. Use your personal Venn diagram as a starting point for the poem. Give your poem a title. The following writing prompt will help you get started:

I used to be _____

But now I am _____

A Class Assembly: People Who Made a Difference

Dragon's Gate beautifully portrays the strength of the human spirit. The Chinese workers who endured the horrendous conditions gave their lives to the transcontinental railroad. In *Dragon's Gate*, Otter stretches his limits and learns the depth of his strength. Most of us never experience the kind of hardship that often tests our inner strength.

Stories of survival are very popular with the public. People feel a greater sense of strength when they learn that ordinary people can be pushed to do extraordinary things. Learn more about the strength of the human spirit and ordinary people who have survived extraordinary circumstances. Find out more about everyday people who have made a difference in the lives of others. Share what you learn with your classmates.

Possible presentation pieces:

- For assembly speakers, invite some of the people interviewed in the earlier lesson "The Strength of the Human Spirit." Have the guests share the struggles they have endured, the means they used to survive, and what they learned about themselves and life from the experience. You could also call various cultural organizations to locate speakers who might be willing to share their experiences (examples—holocaust victims, refugees from the Vietnam War, etc.). You could also ask a relative who was a war veteran to share how he or she survived the experience.

- Research stories from the local papers for the last few months. Try to find those who are local heroes (examples—someone who has rescued somebody else, a firefighter or police officer who handles crises on a daily basis, a person who overcame the odds from an injury or accident, etc.). Ask these people to come share their experiences. If no one is available, students can share their research with the class.

- Create your own presentation piece by studying a person or group of people in history who, through their hardship, courage, or determination made the world a better place. Write a poem, story, or description of what these people did and how they helped change the world.

Chief Joseph   Mother Theresa   Martin Luther King   Helen Keller

- Not everyone does something that makes history. Every day ordinary people do small yet important things that make a difference in the lives of others. Think of someone who has made a difference in your life. Take this opportunity to recognize the special gift of time, energy, or help the individual has given you. Write about why and how he or she has shaped your life. This is a great way to thank someone for what this person has done for you.

Unit Test

Matching: Match the word with the correct definition.

_____	1. stiletto	a.	an addictive drug made from dried poppy juice
_____	2. massacred	b.	a notice, poster, or sign posted in a public place
_____	3. status	c.	a regional form of a language with its own characteristics
_____	4. dialect	d.	slaughtered or killed in great numbers
_____	5. opium	e.	in a lively or stylish manner; with an "attitude"
_____	6. jauntily	f.	souvenir; something kept in order to remember the past
_____	7. defiantly	g.	a poisonous, oily, explosive liquid used in dynamite
_____	8. memento	h.	a knife; a slender dagger
_____	9. nitroglycerine	i.	social standing as viewed by others
_____	10. placard	j.	challenging authority in one's actions or words

True or False: Write "true" if the statement is true in the story. Write "false" if the sentence is not a correct statement about the novel.

_____ 11. Otter was from the group of people called the "Strangers," but he was adopted into a different clan.

_____ 12. Otter kills a Manchu and must hide.

_____ 13. The Chinese workers worked the same hours and received the same pay as other railroad workers doing the same jobs.

_____ 14. Sean, the boss' son, spies on Otter and gives that information to his father.

_____ 15. Otter is humiliated by his cabin mates when he bathes in front of them.

_____ 16. Because of their serious injuries, Doggy and Father both withdraw from everyone.

_____ 17. Because Foxfire is his uncle, Otter is respected and liked.

_____ 18. Otter refuses to leave the mountain when he is given the opportunity to do so.

_____ 19. When the men get their first pay raise, they are angered.

_____ 20. The Chinese workers were honored during the golden spike ceremony.

Comprehension Questions: On a separate piece of paper, write answers to these questions. Write in sentences that show how well you know the story.

21. Why did Otter leave China? (provide at least 2 reasons)

22. Why was the mountain "a place worse than any prison"?

23. What status did the Chinese people have on Tiger Mountain?

24. Why was Kilroy against Sean spending time with Otter?

25. Why did Kilroy whip Otter?

26. Why did Otter choose to stay on the mountain when he hated it so much?

Essay: Choose one of the following statements. Write a detailed explanation to support the statement. Provide evidence for your answer.

27a. Even though Foxfire was not the living legend Otter once thought, Foxfire was a great man.

27b. Otter changed from a weak boy to a strong, daring young man.

Response

Directions: Explain the meanings of these quotations from *Dragon's Gate*. *Italics* indicate where English was spoken in the novel. All other words represent Chinese.

Chapter 4: *"You said the world is changing. I want to see some of it. I want to be part of it."* (page 33)

Chapter 5: "Strange how your life can turn around a single moment. I ask myself, What if I hadn't gone into that restaurant? What if I hadn't made the wish before that? What if I hadn't even gone to see the Dragon's Gate? What if . . . what if?" (page 38)

Chapter 6: "It was strange, but I felt as if a door were being unlocked inside." (page 49)

Chapter 8: "I didn't know it was going to be like this." (page 75)

Chapter 9: "Well, you're riding the Snow Tiger now. And you can't stay on, and you can't get off." (page 77)

Chapter 10: "Get it through your head, boy, or you won't live out a day. In Middle Kingdom, you and I were on top of the heap, but here we're on the bottom. Question the bosses or talk back, and they'll kill you in a dozen different ways." (page 93)

"I shook my head, things still didn't add up. 'You said everyone was free and equal in *America*.' He spread his arms in exasperation. 'They're better in theory than in practice.' " (page 94)

Chapter 14: "I realized with a start that he considered it a comedown for Sean to eat with me — when I had thought it was the opposite. Uncle Foxfire had been all wrong. All westerners might be equal among themselves, but we were not westerners." (page 131)

Chapter 19: "As I held Father's head, Uncle Foxfire began to bind it. 'I swear to you, boy. You'll get down from this mountain and home if it's the last thing I do.' " (page 169)

Chapter 23: "I felt especially bad because of the harsh things I had said to him. He had fallen from being a legend to merely being a man who made mistakes like the rest of us — but even so, I was beginning to realize that he was some kind of man. If I had been him, I would have been sulking in the cabin, unwilling even to go near those who had betrayed me. Whatever I thought of him as a prophet, I had to admire him as a man." (page 196)

Chapter 27: "Once you start guesting, you'll be a guest all your life — whether here or back home." (pages 238–239)

Chapter 28: "I worried that his ghost would have to stay in the wilderness. He would be a guest in death as he had been in life." (page 245)

Chapter 30: " 'I won't forget.' It was a statement. It was a promise." (page 272)

Conversations

In pairs or small groups, write and/or perform the conversations that might have occurred in each of the following situations.

- A group of villagers are awaiting the arrival of Foxfire and Father upon their return from America. Among them are their wives, Lion Rock Lady (Foxfire's wife) and Cassia (Father's wife). (5–7 people)

- Cassia, Father, Foxfire, and Otter are discussing whether Otter should go to America. (4 people)

- Otter and Cricket are in the restaurant where they encounter a drunk Manchu. After asking the man not to sing, Otter finds himself in a fight which leaves the Manchu stabbed with his own knife. (3 people)

- While in hiding, Otter and his Mother discuss his birth parents, his past, and the escape to America. (2 people)

- The trip to America is long, dangerous, and uncomfortable. Many Chinese of different clans are making the arduous journey. The men discuss the conditions with each other. (5 people)

- Sean and Otter meet for the first time on the sledge. During this first encounter, they learn a bit about each other and help each other, too. (3 people — Otter, Sean, driver)

- The young men arrive at the mountain. They are shocked by the realization of what will be their home. (5 people)

- Otter is unhappy about his new place. He cannot understand why Father and Foxfire do not do more to change things. He has not had a chance to see things as they do yet. (3 people)

- Otter and Sean share more about themselves while eating. They learn about cultural differences, including how they each eat, and more about prejudice. (4 people — Sean, Otter, Kilroy, and Dandy)

- Otter defies Kilroy and is whipped. Father tries to stop the situation. Others look on. (5 people — Kilroy, Otter, Father, Foxfire, Sean, Brush)

- Foxfire and Otter are alone on the mountain. When Otter is weak, Foxfire must push him. Later Otter gains more strength and more respect for Foxfire. They learn much about themselves and each other. (2 people)

- The men have had it. They realize that their wages and conditions are far worse than the Americans'. They have been pushed to the limit. Otter leads the men as they walk off the shift. Kilroy and his men are there to stop them, but they do not succeed. (5–7 people: Kilroy, Otter, Doggy, Bright Star, Brush, Keg Mouth, other men)

Bibliography and Related Reading

Fiction

Fraser, Mary Ann. *Ten Mile Day and the Building of the Transcontinental Railroad.* Henry Holt, 1993.

Goble, Paul. *Death of the Iron Horse.* Bradbury, 1987.

Lord, Bette Bao. *In the Year of the Boar and Jackie Robinson.* Harper, 1984.

Wetterer, Margaret K. *Kate Shelly and the Midnight Express.* Carolrhoda Books, 1990.

Wright Group, ed. *Tales of the Far East.* Wright Group, 1988.

Yep, Laurence. *Dragonwings.* Harper and Row, 1975.

Nonfiction

Avery, Derek, ed. *The Complete History of the North American Railroad.* Wellfleet, 1989.

Chiu, Ping. *Chinese Labor in California.* University of Wisconsin, 1969.

Collis, Harry. *American English Idioms.* Passport Books, 1986.

Daley, William. *The Chinese Americans.* Chelsea House, 1987.

Dear, Pamela, ed. *Contemporary Authors.* Vol. 46. Gale Research, 1995.

Fisher, Leonard Everett. *Tracks Across America.* Holiday House, 1992.

Freedman, Russell. *Immigrant Children.* Scholastic, 1992.

Gintzler, A.S. *Rough and Ready Railroaders.* Wright Group, 1994.

Hollingsworth, J.B. *The History of the American Railroad.* Dorset, 1987.

Kranz, Rachel. *Straight Talk about Prejudice.* Facts on File, 1992.

Lee, Kathleen. *Tracing Your Chinese Roots.* Muir, 1993.

Olendorf, Donna, ed. *Something About the Author.* Vol. 69. Gale Research, 1992.

Williams, John Hoyt. *A Great and Shining Road.* Times Books, 1988.

Yep, Laurence. *The Lost Garden; A Memoir by the Author of* Dragonwings. Messner, 1991.

York, Thomas. *North America's Great Railroads.* Dorset, 1987.

Teacher Created Materials

#234 *Immigration* (Thematic Unit)

#282 *Westward Ho* (Thematic Unit)

#295 *Transcontinental Railroad* (Thematic Unit)

#417 *In the Year of the Boar and Jackie Robinson* (Literature Unit)

#429 *Dragonwings* (Literature Unit)

#604 *Survival* (Thematic Unit)

#839 *Teaching Basic Skills Through Literature* (Professional Guide Series)

#843 *Integrating Literature in the Content Areas* (Professional Guide Series)

Answer Key

Page 10

1. to compensate for the fact that he has more than the others; to make them like him rather than resent his good fortune
2. enemies — two centuries before Manchus came and conquered Middle Kingdom — many lives lost
3. regaining power for the Middle Kingdom; ridding it of opium and outside rule; bringing in modern technology in order to create a better place—Accept supported responses.
4. opium; addicting many citizens; many examples of addicts begging or being haggard, etc.
5. village had a sign to represent the movement to overthrow the Manchus — "banish the darkness...restore the light"— rid us of the bad (Manchus, opium, etc.) and bring back the good
6. bring Western technology — steam engine, railroad, improve trade, improve ability to defend
7. struggle between mother, uncle — mom wants Otter to stay, uncle wants Otter to go
8. Otter: stand up to mom, Father: some people are meant to be a followers
9. "I wish that I could join Uncle Foxfire and help him build a better future."
10. the famous gate — erected long ago over river (seems like waterfall); legend — if fish can make long swim upstream, through gate, it will change into dragon; if you want to wish for good luck to someone sitting for the government exams, you give that person a picture of fish swimming through Dragon's Gate
11. Accept any reasonable answers.
12. drunken soldier, argument, fight with Otter because Otter asked him to stop singing — Manchu soldier attacked Otter because he thought Otter was a rebel; in self-defense, Otter pushed soldier away who fell on his own stiletto — Manchu soldier killed — Cricket and Otter run, get in sedan chair — man in chair hides them because his family was raided by Manchus
13. Mother gives him several messages about how he has been raised — not as Stranger; he is from a rebel family, with serpent's blood; Mother also shares details about his birth parents that he has never heard before — helping Otter in his search for his identity.
14. fearful, realization of leaving home

Pages 12–13

1. does not spend much on herself; impatient, independent, does things her own way
2. still has her old, poor country ways
3. does not like fancy things, prefers simplicity, self-conscious about her new financial security
4. had high standards, expectations, control over Otter
5. shows her love for him and what she believes is his destiny
6. her belief in what can and must be inspires hope and purpose in Otter
7. felt that elaborate dressing is wasteful; willing to speak her mind
8. honored, respected by village
9. adventurous, admired
10. some felt he was almost magical — he is legendary
11. powers and abilities have been exaggerated like a tall tale
12. inspires others; Otter wants to follow Uncle's great goals

Page 14

Answers will vary. Some possible examples include:
"I yearned to go someplace where it wouldn't matter what my birth parents had been." (page 4)
"Why should I be the only boy to stay home? ... It would be heaven to be with my father and my uncle, the living legend. Maybe a little glory would settle on me as well." (pages 14-15)
"That's another reason to leave here. You see more and more people taking the demon mud (opium)." (page 14)
"I knew something had to be done very soon for our poor country; and I wanted to be one of those who helped." (page 15)

Page 16

1. month long, packed like coffins, food of rice, vegetables; no privacy; sanitation was using a few buckets; last boat one out of three men died (page 53)
2. left as wasteland; hydraulic mining stripped mountains; tracks gouged big holes, debris left (page 59)
3. escorts got him warm clothing; some family in America; spoke some English (page 54)
4. not dressed warmly enough; Americans in such

Answer Key *(cont.)*

hurry; did not know how to walk (pages 61–73)

5. abusive, alcoholic, mean without booze
(pages 64–68)

6. like a tiger ready to attack; characters frightened by what they see and hear

7. status, privilege, more cooperation (page 76)

8. surprised initially, says letter warning him about winter missed Otter; place worse than prison (pages 82–85)

9. not the hero; lacks status/power; not in charge; must yield to westerner domination

10. Accept reasonable answers.

11. Accept reasonable answers.

12. all people are equal in theory only — in real life not true

13. Accept all valid responses.

14. Accept all valid responses.

15. called Otter a "greenhorn"; Otter had never done hard labor before; makes Chinese workers feel power over someone (pages 102–105)

Page 22

1. Otter is forced to strip and bathe in front of the other men. Father/Foxfire do not want to appear easy on their kin. (pages 118-120)

2. rules helps the men stay healthy; men cannot afford to have a cabin mate get sick and infect the rest, sick mate would also add more labor for the rest (pages 118-120)

3. both parents drank a lot; both took out anger on Sean when booze ran out; Mom did not cook much; moved a lot; mom sick and died; life on mountain better because home life was so inconsistent (pages 127-130)

4. an orphan and from an outcast clan; without his mother's protection, would have been banished from his village or killed (page 128)

5. both young, at odds with their parents, struggling with past; both willing to accept each other even though there is discrimination all around them (pages 126-133)

6. Sean's life is so hard; death looks better to him than life (pages 123, 129)

7. the Chinese men and Sean's father; all felt that everyone should stay with their own kind (pages 130-132)

8. Accept reasonable answers having to do with having a friendship in spite of everyone, doing

things their own way, and rebelling against their fathers. (pages 131-132)

9. to show he would not be easy on his son, to have his son prove his strength; since son lost, Kilroy was angered and humiliated (pages 135-137)

10. wanted California connected to the rest of U.S., felt it would give families a second chance, carry on what his father, grandfather set out to do; Kilroy's dreams like Foxfire's because he felt he, too, could make things better (pages 140-141)

11. guitar stolen and burned for warmth; his music was soothing to all the cabin mates (pages 142-143)

12. Otter organizes men to pitch in whatever they have to get a new guitar for Doggy; he gives up what he has, he organizes the men, he has the inspiration and makes it happen (pages 143-149)

13. Doggy's fingers frostbitten, have to be chopped off; cannot play music and the comfort of his music is missed by all; tragedy also remind them all of how dangerous their lives are (pages 151-153)

14. men start working together as a team, tragedy makes them realize that they have to do all they can to survive, their chances are better if they are together (page 154)

15. Otter wants to hit the mountain badly, he needs a way to vent his rage, hitting the mountain was like hitting the enemy (pages 155-158)

16. need to get as many men out of the tunnel as they can, then could go back for the missing Answers vary. (pages 158-160)

Page 25

Answers will vary. Some ideas include:

1. Privately, I was thinking.

2. Everything is clear-cut — exactly as you see it. There is no overlap or anything in between.

3. You cannot change things right away.

4. I should go.

5. There was a smiling, warm look in his eyes.

6. Doggy plays the guitar.

7. It is time you were doing your share of the work.

8. Let us see how strong you are.

9. You are a coward.

10. Your freedom has been taken; you have been encouraged to drink alcohol.

Answer Key *(cont.)*

Page 27

1. Foxfire can have his dreams; should realize that they hurt others
2. Kilroy shows little sympathy, expects men to continue working
3. to set an example; Answers vary.
4. Answers vary.
5. tries to do all he is still able to do
6. Otter is angry, hurt, and confused
7. feel hopeless, see their lives as expendable
8. Answers vary.
9. Answers vary.
10. Answers vary.
11. Men are afraid; Foxfire wants to save the snow-buried men.
12. Answers vary.
13. take the dangerous trip up the mountain to set the explosives
14. Accept reasonable answers and supported responses.
15. respects Otter, does not have much else in his life, to prove himself to his father

Page 32

1. Accept supported responses. (pages 215, 220)
2. He compares himself to the fish who do not make it. No one blames them and maybe no one will blame Otter if he does not survive the trek up the mountain. (page 217)
3. We have to make things happen for ourselves. (page 218)
4. They understand each other, learn about their own strengths, and learn that maybe they can make a difference, if only a tiny bit at a time. (pages 215-226)
5. Foxfire says he is passing luck onto Otter. The mountain is a beautiful place to die. (pages 227-229)
6. human chain formed of Americans and Chinese to help Otter, gave him food and wood, put him in Foxfire's bunk, back slapped (pages 233-238)
7. must carry on Foxfire's work, must find Foxfire's bones and take them home (page 240)
8. learned about inequities in pay, suffered so much, did not feel much worse could happen (pages 252-253)
9. stronger, braver, leadership qualities developing (pages 253-254)

10. still is not as much as Americans, feels like an insult (page 251)
11. Answers vary.
12. Answers vary.
13. realizes that Foxfire wants him to be his own person, will not want him to waste any more time on mountain (page 267)
14. Chinese were not a part of the golden spike ceremony when the railroad was finally finished; shows the great injustice when the most dangerous work was done by Chinese (page 270)
15. research (pages 273-274)

Page 35

1. relish	5. flounder
2. subscription	6. strike
3. agent	7. resort
4. mess	

Page 42

1. h	11. True
2. d	12. True
3. i	13. False
4. c	14. False
5. a	15. True
6. e	16. False
7. j	17. False
8. f	18. True
9. g	19. True
10. b	20. False

Answers will vary for numbers 21–26. Some possibilities include:

21. to escape punishment; to do the Great Work
22. poor conditions
23. little or no status
24. prejudice, bad influence
25. he wanted to quit working; to set an example to other workers
26. to find Foxfire's bones, to complete Foxfire's work
27a. and b. — Accept answers that provide supporting details.

Page 43

Accept reasonable and supported responses.